I Love Mango!
Marin Mel
Copyright © 2024 by Maring Mel

ISBN 979-8-89383-676-9

Shakei is a happy little girl.
She is five years old. Shakei loves to
dance, sing and play with her toys.

She especially loves her doll Trixie
and her yellow toy car.

Shakei is a joy, and her family
loves her very much.

Shakei is also a very picky eater. She does not like to try new foods.

When her parents would try to get her to eat something new,

"YUCK" would be Shakei's reply. Shakei likes to say "YUCK".

"Shakei, there are so many wonderful
foods to eat. Try something new,
you might like it".
Her parents would say.

"YUCK".
Shakei would yell.
Her parents would
get very frustrated.

Shakei would eat cereal
and pizza all the time
if her parents would
allow it.

One Sunday afternoon,
Shakei's grandmother
came over to visit.

Grandma always brought gifts
for her family.

This time she brought
mangoes for everyone.

Grandma and Shakei sat
and had a chat as they
usually did.

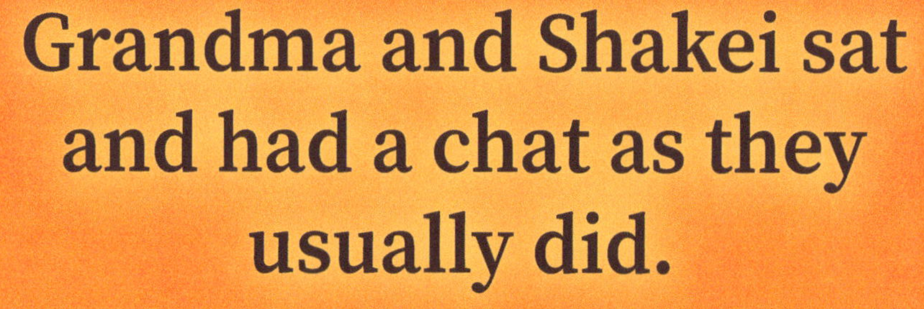

Grandma started to eat a mango.
She used her teeth to
remove the mango peels.

It was ripe and sweet and juicy.
"HMM" was all grandma said
as she ate her mango.

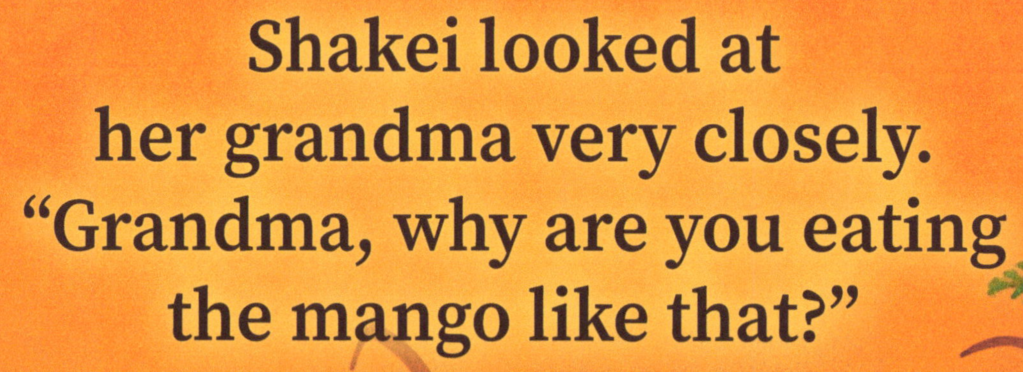

Shakei looked at
her grandma very closely.
"Grandma, why are you eating
the mango like that?"

"Because I wanted to eat it" grandma
replied not looking up from
her tasty mango.

"But you did not use a knife" Shakei said
sounding very confused.
"You can use a knife but when I was a
little girl like you, this is how I ate mangoes".
Grandma said with a smile.

"It looks like fun",
Shakei said excitedly.
"Yes it is", grandma said, lost
in her tasty, tropical treat.

Shakei took a mango and
followed grandma, who was now
on her second mango.
Grandma and Shakei sat
and ate their mangoes.
"Hmm" is all they said.
Shakei's mom came into the room
and was in awe of what she saw.
She smiled at the sight of her
mom and daughter eating happily.

After a while there were mango peels
and mango juice everywhere.
Her shirt had yellow mango stains
all over it. Shakei put her mango pit
down and with a burst of excitement,
threw her hands up and shouted,

Shakei was overjoyed she jumped up
with her mango-stained hands and said
"Mom, mom, can I have mango later on
and tomorrow, and for my birthday?"

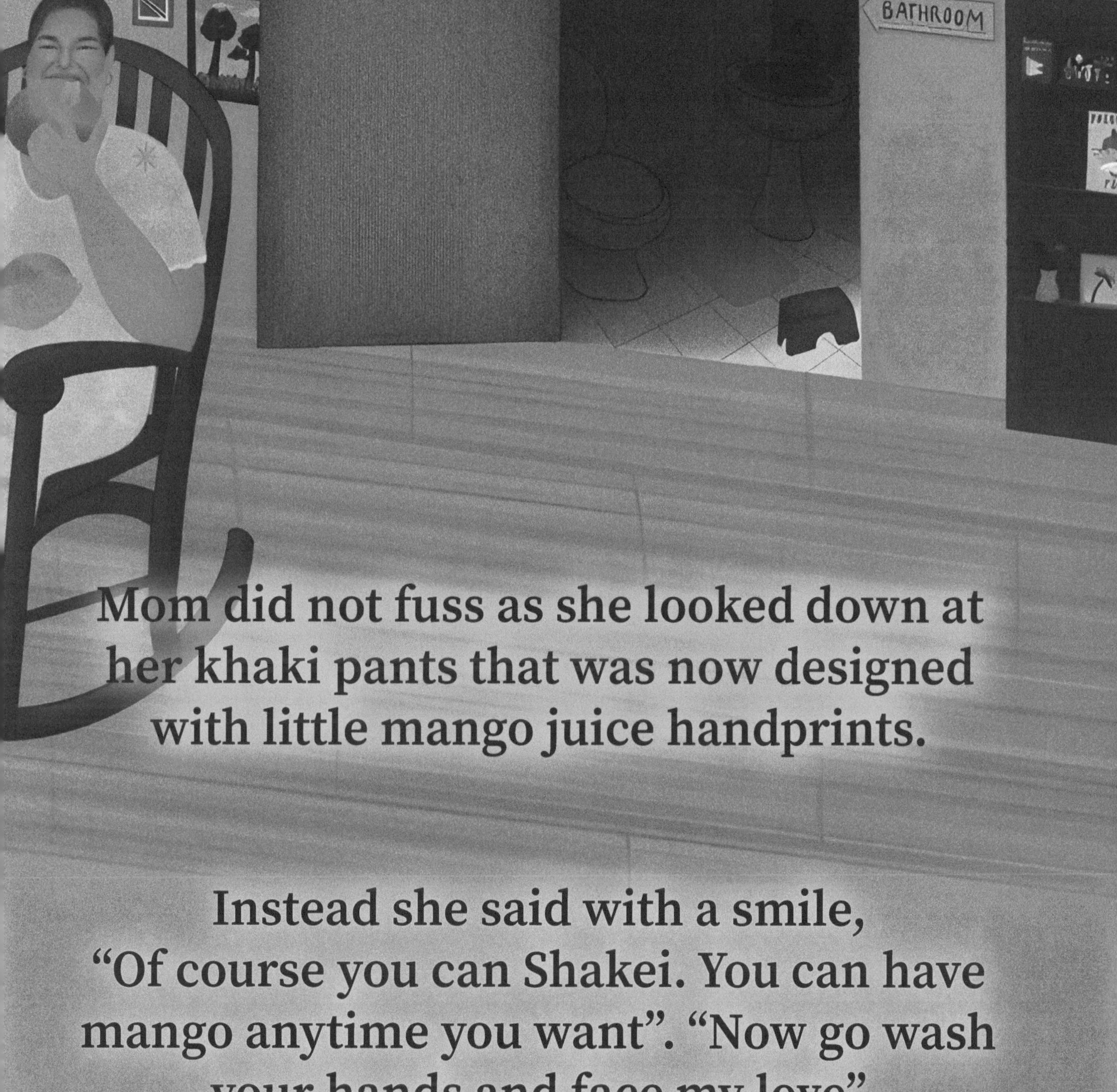

Mom did not fuss as she looked down at her khaki pants that was now designed with little mango juice handprints.

Instead she said with a smile, "Of course you can Shakei. You can have mango anytime you want". "Now go wash your hands and face my love"

"Mom, how did you get
Shakei to try
something new?"

"How did you get her to eat a mango?"
Shakei's mom really wanted to know.

"I did not do anything; I just sat
here enjoying my mangoes".
"She was looking at me, then
she asked me why I peeled
the mango with my teeth. The next
thing I knew, she was eating
her own" Grandma replied.

"Just like that?" Shakei's mom asked.
"Yes, just like that" grandma replied.

Shakei returned with her doll Trixie.
"Grandma, can Trixie have a mango too?"
Shakei asked with a smile.

In her best Trixie voice, Shakei said:
"I love mango"
Shakei was also a funny kid.
Everyone laughed and laughed.

From that day foward, Shakei's
parents did not get frustrated
that she was a picky eater.
They realized that she would learn to
eat new things when she was ready.
Shakei got better at trying new foods
because she tried mangoes
on her own and she loves it.
Shakei is a smart girl.

As time went by, Shakei
learned to like new foods and
rarely said YUCK.
She still wanted pizza
and cereal sometimes.
But her new favorite food
was mango.

THE
END